ALL THOSE RAGGED SCARS

ALL THOSE RAGGED SCARS

Sonja Johanson

Choose the Sword
P R E S S

Published by choose the sword press
Hayward, California

© 2015 Sonja Johanson

All Rights Reserved
Published in the United States of America

ISBN10: 0692518916
ISBN13: 978-0692518915

Cover Image: charles taylor/Shutterstock

read a fuckin' book
www.ctspress.com

Contents

Hamako

"...he is in a place he has never seen before." Tejima

Wool, leather, down - if you can take it from an animal, you will. Fox tracks wander in the snow, lose the straight way up the mountain. You can't know why they circle here, why they go into the woods, or not, how those tracks can suddenly end with no explanation, as though the fox was minding its own business, snuffling the perfume of tunneling field mice, when all at once it was the rapture for that little vulpine. This might be Reynard, come at night, casing the barnyard, looking for buckets of chicken but settling for rice pudding. This might be a funeral where skywriters make clouds from the guest of honor, where we toss about Hiroshima, talk back to cops, rattle the magic abacus. It might even be the girl fox you watched leaping in the field, when you were just a vixen yourself, when the sun was so gold on her brown skin and your red fur, before the pines grew in. You'll never know.

The Nightmother

smells of powdered steel. With bastard
file, diamond stone,
whetstone, rasp, she
sharpens fragile

edges. Tying back the bindings,
she lays hot iron
against base, smokes
fragrant paraffin.

Wax shavings settle, clouds, around
her ankles. Day
break, we fasten
blades to our feet.

Car Pool after Band Practice, Monday Nights

The band room.
Where anyone could go, even
the ugly, even the unpopular,
and they would take you in.
Even the kids without talent,
if you would sing or beat
a drum, they'd take you.

They'd take you in the cinder-
block and brick linoleum
fortress, you who wouldn't
ever have a future, you who
no one would ever love, would
have no children, you who

waited in the four o'clock dark,
wind racing through your thin
jacket, waving goodbye to flutes
and trumpets, waving off the synth
and sexy bass, walking home
alone after everyone had gone.

Believer

Some people, I know
have a God-shaped
hole in their heart. They
suck on faith like an empty
socket, breath whistling
where belief used to sit.

Not me.
When I knew Jesus
he was always last kid
picked – couldn't hit
a curve ball, much less
feed a hungry crowd.

You can't tell me
we could count on
any kind of father.

Three Sheets

Is really a way of not knowing
what to do, or where to go,
abandoned, riding the danger
of the jetty breakers, dreaming
of bonfires, musty shacks, oxbows.

It's most of your judgment loosened,
seduced by phosphorescent footsteps,
the sails making their own poor decisions.

After you've been unmoored
by too many shots of Malibu, driftwood
floating on the rollers, the tangerine
sun, a tambourine of spare change,
it's hard to let some sailor tie you down.

Blackberries

Crawling through cool tunnels between the canes, grass soaking through your jeans, dodging thorns and hunting berries in their fat clusters, hanging thick as grapes, but softer, so soft they dissolve on fingertips, they have to be taken, sweet and bleeding, on the tongue, like a lover whose own skin was broken once, or more than once, who can never forget that pain, it comes back sometimes, shuddering strong, something like pleasure the memory that rips the covers off who you are now and lays you raw before the person you want to have and the person you want to be, sobbing fear you try to bury and wish would go away but it never does, you can only hope to shield your lover from the spines and offer up the tart black fruit of who it made you, hope the harvest is worth the work and all those ragged scars.

Everybody Gets to Write an Aubade

it's supposed to be about how you finally
found the lover you were always meant
to have and you both are tangled together
while you watch her sleeping and the sun
better not come up this morning because
the world or fate or karma owes you a little
more time to keep everything this perfect

but maybe yours is about how you
stood on the driveway and didn't do
anything when you really wanted to
and then you just walked away like
a putz and twenty years later you
can't get to sleep because of it so
you're looking for her on facebook

and maybe sue's is about how she was
so supportive and understanding but
the guy was always a gambler or a drunk
or otherwise fucked up and nothing ever
really worked out and so at fifty she's still
waiting red-eye tables during hunting season
even though she knows she's better than this

and maybe mine is about those
times when you hope for something
but you're not sure if it's there and
how you don't dare to say anything
because if you don't mention it maybe
it will happen but if you do mention it
probably it will fly out the window

Morning After

the space between *just going for a few drinks,*
be back and *waking up cradling your cell*
phone in your hands is wild and varied

for days you don't want anyone,
forgiveness is a mystery, untenable;
your throat begins to spasm

mid-sentence, your tongue seizes, fingers
curl into frozen claws, painless but
disturbing, like pulling on a loaded wire

wild swans

always, I'm a witch
or some similar word

whatever it takes to keep me
silent and sleeping with you

work in the textile mills
till my hands are ruined

blackface, so you can call
me other, throw me out

but walnut husks have
their own perfume

dreadlocks are in –
haven't you heard?

and nettle soup is all the rage
with wild-foraging locavores

glass, iron, stone, it's been
worn smooth, been mingled

today, I found eleven
white feathers by the ocean

tomorrow, I will give away
winter coats to the homeless

you can keep your piety -
I left mine in the churchyard

The Girl Doesn't Know Her Ozymandius From Her Kubla Khan

She wakes up already manic, she's like
a god who's daughter is a big headache.
It's a migraine rattling around her skull,
she's crazy to get it out, she knocks down
two Sudafed and chugs a Red Bull, draws
a broken statue and a bunch of sand.

He comes back from getting coffee, she's called
in sick again. She's blasting Morrison
at 10 a.m., turpentine all over.
Numbers ripple up and down her biceps-
racing stripes. He wants to wash them off. He's
a god who's daughter is a big headache.

She tells him she remembers from her dream;
she's in some pleasure-dome, there's a river
of dark water where she spilled the coffee.
He turns on ESPN until she hollers
that he has to keep that noise down.
It's a migraine rattling around her skull.

The room's a cavern. She's burning incense;
smoke hangs over her palate, her garden.
The cat sidles through the earth-tone flowers,
jumps on the table, bats at the brushes.
Jesus Christ, why would he let the cat in,
she's crazy to get it out, she knocks down

the lamp. Lightbulb shrapnel is everywhere.
He cleans it up. She's daubing taupe like mud,
it's almost done, she's gonna sell this one
maybe for a million bucks and they'll get
a decent place to stay. She's wrong. He takes
two Sudafed and chugs a Red Bull, draws

his breath in, wants to have a Marlboro.
She lights one up; it's afterglow for her.
He kicks the dropcloth hard against the wall.
This one's the dumbest thing he's ever seen.
He inhales raw paint and tells her "It's just
a broken statue and a bunch of sand."

The Pumpkin Thinks

/Pumpkins don't think
Be accurate with your words/
The pumpkin wants to last as long as it can -
/Be impeccable/
The pepo is the cucurbitacean mechanism for seed dispersal.
/That's better Go on/
Cucurbits have evolved for vernal germination.
/Excellent Now what?/
The pumpkin sees the other pumpkins rotting
/Stay on task/
Under ideal conditions, mature fruits remain intact until spring,
minimizing opportunities for disease or predation.
/What evolutionary pressure drives this adaptation?/
The pumpkin would be happier if you
were in your shirt sleeves The pumpkin
would like to winter in the Bahamas The
pumpkin appreciates the occasional pina
colada
/Skip to the next part please/
Pepos which decompose concurrently with ideal germination
time tables maximize offspring survival rates.
/So how would you explain all this to a layman?/
The pumpkin believes that it can float
all the way to Molokai, and that it would
prefer a luau to Halloween The pumpkin
is unwilling wear rings to stretch its neck
like some butternut, have its feet bound,
or be hired as a baby mama Find yourself
another squash The pumpkin quits

Blanket

The only thing
worth anything
in a blaze –

soak it and filter
the smoke from
your lungs, wrap

it like a cloak
and toss off
the flames, roll

up in it and crush
out oxygen, use it
to beat the flickering

tongues from another
person. The only
thing I have from

you; the only thing
I'll take with me if
this life catches fire.

Taste for Bitter

Our parents place honey
on our tongues at our first letter,
teaching us to love sugar as much as books.
We are bribed with lollipops, rewarded
with cupcakes, told we have a right
to pursue sweetness.

But when the adults are not watching,
we delight in sucking on secret lemons,
forage the edges for wood sorrel, sneak
into the neighbor's orchard for the sharp
bite of Rhode Island Greening -
using sour as a gateway flavour.

As adults, we desperately offer
our children the sweetness that
is lost to us. Diminished by
the monotony of our desks, watching
dully as our partners recede, we develop
a fondness for broccoli raab.

We welcome the herbs on the Seder
plate, the alkaloid kiss of balsam apple.
Made curious by the burst of orange oil
we drag our lips across illicit skin,
accidentally taste our own perfume,
and find it to our liking.

Why I Can't Write

The last time I was here someone
posted the word "pluviophile". I'd
have done anything - anything –

ordered men's flannel nightshirts,
black watch; license plates; street
signs; oil companies; colleges.

There was such charming grass
in the New Scotland cemetery,
and I so longed to nap between

the sunny headstones that I shut
the door for twenty years. I had to
switch over to coffee, the opening

notes of the Intermezzi putting me
off my salad. There were day trips
to the extreme north Hebrides, your

name was everywhere, on a bookstore
called "Muse", just "Muse", a horrible
joke, but there was nothing to be done.

Footloose

I set free all the odd socks - the whole jumbled
mismatched basket of them. Perky, purple girl ones
with their tattoo patterns; black and navy dress socks
you couldn't tell apart; an enormous herd
of white cotton ones, all sizes. So many years
spent guarding and sorting by age, colour, material,
owner, size. Patiently watching for missing mates
that the dryer long ago chewed to lint.

But I had to admit it was time to let them go.
I made sure that they were dry and clean,
stroked their fuzzy wool, then tucked them
in their basket, and drove to a nice spot
in the country. I lifted the lid and watched
them slip away. The house is so quiet now.

In Temple Grandin, I Find a Kindred Soul

I sit at the dock's edge,
the small pond rocked by speed boats,
wakes which overpower its dimensions.

Behind me, the Terhi, tied to its cleats
is lifted and dropped by the swells.
On each rise it rides hard up my spine
drags down as the water recedes.

I am comforted by this,
as if I am mucking the barn
while the old horse in the next stall
nudges me, repeatedly
with his long, bony nose
in hopes of an extra ration.

The boat offers the confident attentions
of an experienced partner
who knows me well enough
to dispense with juvenile gentleness.

Full Shade

Today, she aches. She wakes with the long stretch
of groaning belly and back, the howl of inner thighs

unused to slaving, fingertips ripped by thorns.
Yesterday, all day was spent crouching, weeding

the shady soil she had ignored for so many summers.
Toad-lilies revealed themselves behind the crunch

of jewelweed stems; ramps, planted before
her third child came to take her time, shot

up minute scapes. No one knows the things
which grow in the beautiful dark, the lungwort,

wood poppies, swaths of bloodroot advancing
out of mind. She opens the garden, remembering.

In the Church of the Holy Coffee Bean

business plans unfold, spreadsheets
spill off the table. Newspapers migrate
from person to person, a shared offering.

Couples gaze, those who should and those
who shouldn't; tearful mothers, desperate
for stimulation both chemical and human,
ply toddlers with sippy cups and pastries.

We the regular parishioners, offer our daily
tithing. We kneel beneath paintings of Latino
saints who smile and harvest bright red berries.

We breathe in roasty incense, notes of tamari,
smoke, peanut butter. We bow our heads before
the high baristas, chant *cappuccino, espresso,*
macchiato, reverently sip the hot black heaven.

Grass Widow

One day you look up and there has
been a terrible mishap in the kitchen -
an entire glass of Chardonnay has spilled
directly into the palm of your hand.

You clean the mess, swallow after swallow,
wondering where your husband is.
You are pretty sure you have a husband
but who can tell, what with the split-

level empty days, evenings
bookended on the sofa, the dim
feeling that your mailman may be
judging you. What business of his

if you take in plain brown packages,
vaguely phallic? It is raining
as you have another accident of wine,
but we aren't talking about love

on a roof in Brooklyn, you are only
weaving all that gold into a bed of straw.

Brimstone

The bitter night house, hands
stiff with radiant cold and bones.
Birchbark, white pine twigs, dry

split ash. Just one strike, one fast
pop, sinuses quick with sulfur vapour,
breathing in the salt marsh on fire,

praying for the catch of tinder, kindling,
praying in winter that the whole box,
the whole yellow forest could light up.

Acknowledgments

Thanks to the following journals for giving these poems their first home:

The Avocet Weekly: "Brimstone"
Cider Press Review: "wild swans"
The Gambler: "The Pumpkin Thinks"
Kind of a Hurricane Press: "In the Church of the Holy Coffee
    Bean"
Kudzu: "Blanket", "Blackberries (Kudzu Poetry Prize)"
Poetry Breakfast: "Footloose", "Full Shade"
Red Headed Stepchild: "Grass Widow"
Referential: "Hamako"
Revolution John: "Everybody Gets to Write an Aubade"
Shot Glass Journal: "In Temple Grandin, I Find a Kindred
    Soul"
The Unrorean: "The Girl Doesn't Know Her Ozymandius
    from Her Kubla Khan", "The Nightmother",
    "Taste for Bitter", "Three Sheets"

Bio

Sonja Johanson attended College of the Atlantic, in Bar Harbor, ME. She currently serves as the outreach coordinator for the Massachusetts Master Gardener Association. She has recent work appearing in The Albatross, the Nonbinary Review, and Off the Coast, is a contributing editor at the Found Poetry Review, and is the recipient of the 2015 Zero Bone Poetry and Kudzu Poetry Prizes. Sonja divides her time between work in Massachusetts and her home in the mountains of western Maine.